a pocketful of
RHYME
Imagination for a new generation

2006 Poetry Competition for 7-11 year-olds

YoungWriters

Co Durham Verses
Edited by Angela Fairbrace

 Young**Writers**

First published in Great Britain in 2007 by:
Young Writers
Remus House
Coltsfoot Drive
Peterborough
PE2 9JX
Telephone: 01733 890066
Website: www.youngwriters.co.uk

SB ISBN 1 84602 754 3

Foreword

Young Writers was established in 1991 and has been passionately devoted to the promotion of reading and writing in children and young adults ever since. The quest continues today. Young Writers remains as committed to the nurturing of poetic and literary talent as ever.

This year's Young Writers competition has proven as vibrant and dynamic as ever and we are delighted to present a showcase of the best poetry from across the UK and in some cases overseas. Each poem has been selected from a wealth of *A Pocketful Of Rhyme* entries before ultimately being published in this, our fourteenth primary school poetry series.

Once again, we have been supremely impressed by the overall quality of the entries we have received. The imagination, energy and creativity which has gone into each young writer's entry made choosing the poems a challenging and often difficult but ultimately hugely rewarding task - the general high standard of the work submitted ensured this opportunity to bring their poetry to a larger appreciative audience.

We sincerely hope you are pleased with this final collection and that you will enjoy *A Pocketful Of Rhyme Co Durham Verses* for many years to come.

Contents

Bishop Ian Ramsey CE School
Christopher Heafield (10)   1
Azeria Robson (10)   2
Nathan Weighill (10)   3
Ellen Chambers (10)   4
Fiona Back (10)   5
Emily Elsy (10)   6

Cockfield Primary School
Ashleigh Teasdale (10)   7
Katie Gipps (10)   8
Michael Briton (9)   9
Kyle Pattison (9)   10
Sam Sawden (10)   11
Ryan Anderson (10)   12
Elliot Herring (9)   13
Bethany Watson (9)   14
Georgina Blyth (9)   15
Ben Robinson (9)   16
Chloe Slater (10)   17
Jake Cummings (10)   18
Hannah Kirkby (9)   19
Daniel Jenkins (9)   20
Keziah Peel (10)   21
Phoebe Walker (11)   22
Nicole Walton (9)   23

Dean Bank School
Cameron Watson (8)   24
Issac Pearson (8)   25
Jacqueline Walker (8)   26
Amy Hopper (8)   27
James McCarthy (8)   28
Christopher Palin (8)   29
Jordan Walton (8)   30
Brendan (8) & Jake Riseley (9)   31
Lee Sheavils (8)   32
Jessica Upton (8)   33
Jacob Galpin (8)   34

Matthew Limon (8)	35
Rachael Farley (8)	36
Nathan Wilson (8)	37
Connor Pearson (8)	38
Caitlyn Atkinson (8)	39
Ewan Redhead (9)	40

East Stanley School

Liam Bailey (7)	41
Rhiannon Quinn (7)	42
Ewan Taws (7)	43
Emily Chambers (7)	44
Joel Hall (8)	45
Lucy Bates (7)	46
Michael McNally (7)	47
Reece Jefferson (7)	48
Ben Murphy (7)	49
Callum Boakes (7)	50
Stephen Chan (7)	51
Summer Thompson (7)	52
Chloe Macallister (8)	53
Georgia Kent (7)	54
Sean Spinks (7)	55
Emma Pickering (8)	56
Jade Bell (8)	57
Aiden Brown (7)	58
Abigail Keall (7)	59
Kirsty Barnwell (8)	60
Alicia Mallon (7)	61
Ryan Lister (7)	62
Aaron Richardson (8)	63
Eleanor Haswell (10)	64
Ryan Bell (10)	65
Dean Swinbank (10)	66
Samantha Appleby (10)	67
James Blanchard (10)	68
Hannah Emmerson (10)	69
Ben Storey (9)	70
Jessica Bates (10)	71
Dominic Cox (10)	72
Shannon Gray (9)	73

Dean Greaves (9)   74
Andrew Nealen (9)   75
Molly Cruddas (9)   76

Middlestone Moor Primary School
Conrad Ashton (10)   77
Jade Lawlor (10)   78
Jamie Longthorne (10)   79
Katie O'Rourke (10)   80
Liam Daglish (10)   81
Bethany Gulliver (10)   82
Alexander Tonge (10)   83
Zoe Hauxwell (11)   84
Kieran Kyle (10)   85
Leanne Pearson (10)   86
Alex Close (10)   87
Sarah Barnes (11)   88
Jordan Palmer (11)   89
James Foreman (10)   90
Hannah Gulliver (10)   91
Stacey Doughty (10)   92
Marcus Brownless (10)   93
Ryan Whitehead (10)   94
Chloe Smith (10)   95
Kelly Cooney (10)   96

Mowden Junior School
J J Adair (8)   97
Eleanor Andrews (9)   98
Olivia Hugill (8)   99
Richard Smith (8)   100
Jack Cooper (8)   101
Tyler Skelton (8)   102
Jack Norcup (8)   103
Caitlin Stabler (8)   104
Jonathon Dent (8)   105
James Marshall (8)   106
Daniel Crane (8)   107
Hollie Sanderson (8)   108
Emily Carroll (8)   109
Ben McMain (9)   110

David Wilcock (9)   111
Josh O'Brien (8)   112
Thomas Richard Rayner (8)   113
Eleanor Bairstow (8)   114
Hayley Howard (9)   115
Georgia Broadbent (9)   116
Jake Powely (8)   117
Holly Marks (8)   118
Thomas Peter William McDonald (8)   119
Emma McGarrell (8)   120
Luke Hutchinson (8)   121
Lucy Hodgson (8)   122
Laura Whitehouse (9)   123
Kieran Joel Harman Spencer (9)   124
Bethany John (8)   125
Sophie Naisbitt (8)   126
Chris Vardy (8)   127
Callam Luke Jobling (8)   128
Callum Gault (8)   129
Ellie Louise Lawson (8)   130
Michael John English (8)   131
Emma Raine (8)   132
Tom O'Brien (8)   133
John Lorimer (8)   134
Hannah Caitlin Alderson (9)   135
Thomas William Armstrong (8)   136
Patrick Burney (8)   137
Kathryn Haynes (8)   138
Joshua Bynoe (10)   139
Alex Miller (10)   140
Crystelle Challands (11)   141
Selina Todd (10)   142
Katherine Louise Armstrong (10)   143
Samuel Howard (10)   144
Humza Malik (10)   145
Hannah Jenkinson (10)   146
Matthew Crane (11)   147
Fiona Lupton (10)   148
Elizabeth Oliver (11)   149
Hannah Dennis (11)   150
Jordan Moohan (11)   151
Hayley Soanes (11)   152

Jonathan O'Neill (10)	153
Michael Bell (10)	154
Danielle Wright (11)	155
Katie Finch (10)	156
Robyn Colling (10)	157
Lauren Jordinson (10)	158
Chloe Newsome (10)	159
Lucy Dawson (10)	160
Jack Stephen Raine (10)	161
Stephanie Wilson (10)	162
Harry Brockbanks (10)	163
Sarah Ingham (10)	164
Ben Donaldson (11)	165
Ellie May (10)	166
Harriet Donald (10)	167
Maddy Wood (10)	168
Amy McLay (10)	169
Jennifer English (11)	170
Isabel Walker (10)	171
Robert Lawson (10)	172
Daneille Murdock (10)	173
Sophie Gowling (10)	174
Matthew West (10)	175
Erin Watson (10)	176

Sacriston Junior School

Daniel Aydon (8)	177
Paige Calcutt (8)	178
Thomas West (8)	179
Samantha Roseberry (8)	180
Taylor-Jayne Johnson (8)	181
Matthew Buil (9)	182
Joseph French (9)	183
Megan Weldon (8)	184
Paige Birnie (8)	185
Alexandra Campbell (9)	186
Conor Robson (8)	187
Zac Wright (8)	188
Laura Wilkinson (8)	189
Joshua Beacham (8)	190
Elysia Scott (8)	191

Sarah Lamb (8)   192
Tomas Bussey (11)   193

Sugar Hill Primary School
Aaron Hetherington (11)   194
Jake Marshall (9)   195
Caitlin Hindle (9)   196
Lois Rivers (9)   197
Jack Smart (9)   198

The Poems

Dragons

In the air I see, Dreadful fire
It's buRning all the telephone wire

It flies like an eAgle
Better than a seaGull

It's got a kind of fire hOse
That's really just its Nose

It's got an ugly Face
The manners are a dIsgrace

It has Red shiny scales
Which glistEn in its trails.

Christopher Heafield (10)
Bishop Ian Ramsey CE School

My Poem

Fairies, monsters, ghosts and ghouls,
Magic, power, goblins, toons,

Fairies frolic through the air,
They do not want to stare,
Playing all day through the trees,
Whispers are heard in the breeze,

Monsters seize you by the leg,
They trip up on a peg,
Monsters hide under your bed,
They do not need to be fed.

Ghosts know you're in for a scare,
They don't actually pair,
Doom they will bring to you all,
They are really, really tall,

Ghouls are just the same as ghosts,
They actually have toasts,
Feeling their way through the house,
They are not scared of a mouse,

Magic sawing through the sky,
It does not shower nigh,
Swerving to and fro up high,
It always is having a fly,

Power strong no power weak,
Power light but it's meek,
Finding it hard is to see,
Understand, it's not like tea,

All these things here and there,
Let's just say they're everywhere!

Azeria Robson (10)
Bishop Ian Ramsey CE School

WWE

Undertaker is very tall
Rey Mysterio is very small

Vito wears a dress
Umaga is a mess

Batista is very muscly
King Booker is hustly

Matt Hardy is great
Jeff Hardy does the twist of fate

Edge does the spear
Kane has no fear.

Nathan Weighill (10)
Bishop Ian Ramsey CE School

Witch, Witch

Witch . . . witch, where do you go?
'Do you really need to know?'

Witch . . . witch, where do you eat?
'Down the road to Hurricane Street!'

Witch . . . witch, what do you drink?
'A little potion called bloody ink!'

Witch . . . witch, where do you sleep?
'Up in the clouds without a peep!'

Witch . . .witch, how do you fly?
'You don't need to know, just up in the sky!'

Ellen Chambers (10)
Bishop Ian Ramsey CE School

The Sea

Salty water, seaweed too,
Fish swimming in the deep, dark blue
Thin ones, fat ones as well
It's much better than searching in a well
The white shark and jellyfish
Killer whale and catfish
Puffer fish, blue shark and hake
This is what the sea will make
Coral reefs and shiny shells
You can sometimes hear the sound of bells
Dolphins and whales making a great big splash
Some other creatures like to mash
So if you go down there
Do be aware
And do take a light
As it's not very bright
Salty water and seaweed too
Fish swimming in the deep, dark blue.

Fiona Back (10)
Bishop Ian Ramsey CE School

Fairy Tales

Fairy tales are full of romance and love,
Witches and fairies come from above.
They're all make-believe or so it would seem,
Unicorns and goblins all in one dream,
But this is a land where magic is scattered,
And all your problems would be shattered.
Lurking between those frightful thorns,
Pixies and witches and white unicorns,
Mermaids and castles with tumbling stone,
Walking skeletons with white crumbled bone,
Double, bubble, toil and trouble,
Cauldrons and spells, witches that huddle,
Sparkling wings and party hats,
Goblins and giants, white and black cats,
Now it's the morning, it's time to wake,
All those dreams, it was all fake,
But now I know what fairy tales are
I believe in fairies now by far.

Emily Elsy (10)
Bishop Ian Ramsey CE School

I'll Follow You

I'll follow you anywhere,
Down rabbit holes,
Or a fox's lair,
Misty dew,
Through raging blizzarding snow,
I'll follow you wherever you go.
Round a castle moat,
Down the field to the sea,
Take a boat will you and me,
Through heavy storms and raging seas,
To a place that has a gentle breeze.
I'll follow you through,
Blazing deserts and frozen Iceland,
Pyramids, temples, safari park,
I'll even follow you in the dark
Whatever the climate,
I'll be there,
I'll follow you,
And watch all you do.

Ashleigh Teasdale (10)
Cockfield Primary School

I'll Follow You

I'll follow you around in the rain, on the path, through the trees to
the school.

I'll follow you through snow, through bliss and despair,
Where you go I will be there.

I'll follow you when you go through the thunder and lightning,
Wherever you go I will be there watching.

I'll follow you through the desert, through the snow,
I will be with you wherever you go.

I'll follow you beyond the weather.
I'll follow you until we are together.

Katie Gipps (10)
Cockfield Primary School

I'll Follow You

I'll follow you through the pale ticket gates.
I'll follow you down the cold concrete alleys.
I'll follow you to your seat.
I'll follow you to watch the match.
At half-time I'll follow you to the pie stand.
I'll follow you to the exit of the ground.
I'll follow you all around.

Michael Briton (9)
Cockfield Primary School

I Saw

I saw an ant, growling at a fox.
I saw a bear, standing on a bookshelf.
I saw a wet heart, ticking away.
I saw a clock, falling off a plane.
I saw a piece of paper, fly to Australia.
I saw a bird, smelling its way through.
I saw a stink bug, with seven humps.
I saw a camel, electrocuting me.
I saw a piece of wire, crawling along.

Kyle Pattison (9)
Cockfield Primary School

I'll Follow You

I'll follow you in a hot lava cave where magma splats all over the floor.
I'll follow you past fiery red dragons and around bubbles of magma
And under stalactites like deadly spears.
I'll follow you beneath ceilings of hard jagged rock
And across a hard rock bridge with lava under it
And I'll follow you past crimson walls.
I'll follow you past deadly alive skeletons.
I'll follow you beyond and beneath the deep blue ocean
And past the deadly bloodthirsty sharks.
I'll follow you wherever you are!

Sam Sawden (10)
Cockfield Primary School

I'll Follow You

I'll follow you across the wonky beans' aisle and the bleeping tills.
I'll follow you, past the alcohol aisle and around the sweet aisles
Where the children are getting their treats.
I'll follow you, where there are fizzy drinks, where the fish aisle stinks,
I'll follow you where the crisps stand straight on the shelves.
I'll follow you, past the tins of peas.
I'll follow you, past the milk and the butter.
I'll follow you, through the meat aisle.
I'll follow you, over the fruit.
I'll follow you across the vegetables.
I'll follow you, nasty brute.

Ryan Anderson (10)
Cockfield Primary School

What Are . . .

What are hairy? Dogs and cats.
What are cold? Milk and ice.
What are sharp? Daggers and grass.
What are slimy? Snails and slugs.

Elliot Herring (9)
Cockfield Primary School

I'll Follow You

I'll follow you going down the silent wards.
I'll follow you in the lifts and down the stairs.
I'll follow you where the needles lay in the doctor's drawer.
I'll follow you under the terrible room of the operating table.
I'll follow you where X-rays are taken.
I'll follow you where water drips from the taps.
I'll follow you with the knives smothered in blood.
I'll follow you wherever you go.
I'll follow you with a rotten toe.

Bethany Watson (9)
Cockfield Primary School

I Saw

I saw a cute teddy, full with water.
I saw a shiny bottle, eating its food.
I saw a blonde dog, using an umbrella.
I saw an old lady, shiny and gold.
I saw a new cup, brown and tall.
I saw a young horse, stripy and colourful.
I saw an England cap, sharp and pointy.
I saw this letter, soft and cosy.

Georgina Blyth (9)
Cockfield Primary School

The Question

Did dinosaurs exist?
How do things grow?
Who made up all the names of things?
Why do dogs bite?
Who named the colours?
Which came first, the chicken or the egg?
How much water is in the sea?
How many cm of earth are there?

Ben Robinson (9)
Cockfield Primary School

I Saw

I saw a pig, bite the postman.
I saw a dog, scratching away.
I saw a cat, go into a small house.
I saw a guinea pig, make an invention.
I saw a man, flying up high.
I saw a bird, stay underwater for a lifetime.
I saw a whale, crawl up the drainpipe.
I saw a spider, oink away.

Chloe Slater (10)
Cockfield Primary School

I Saw

I saw a bucket, salty and crunchy.
I saw salt and vinegar crisps, moving along.
I saw a white house, reading The Beano.
I saw myself, all noisy and loud.
I saw my television, with racing games.
I saw a computer, open its body.
I saw a brand new toy, full of sand.

Jake Cummings (10)
Cockfield Primary School

I'll Follow You

I'll follow you through different weathers, rainy, stormy, sunshine,
snow and wind!
I'll follow you through deserts, red-hot, and cold ice that lies there
every year!
I'll follow you through stormy seas, through sharks and fish that kill!
I'll follow you through sunny cities and villages that are still!
I'll follow you through coal, red-hot and rocks freezing cold!
I'll follow you through dead bodies that have frozen!
I'll follow you through sharp wind and storms and rain!
I'll follow you through frozen birds and swans!

Hannah Kirkby (9)
Cockfield Primary School

What Are . . .

What are clever?
Brains and children.

What are cold?
Milk and ice.

What are harsh?
People and words.

Daniel Jenkins (9)
Cockfield Primary School

I'll Follow You

I'll follow you,
Past the trees and into shops,
By the shoes, lots and lots.
I'll follow you,
Through skirts and scarves,
If anything gets in my way
I'll cut them in half.
I'll follow you,
Into the café where the waitress
Says, 'What can I get you
Today?'
I'll follow you,
You can't go far
I'll get you wherever you are!

Keziah Peel (10)
Cockfield Primary School

I'll Follow You

I'll follow you through shops and stalls,
By the clothes aisle and more and more,
Past burger bars and into phone shops,
Like Phones 4 You,
I'll follow you over ramps
Past high-heeled shoes, pink handbags,
And plenty more,
I'll follow you through sports shops,
JJB and Megurks,
I'll follow you around watch stalls,
Into toilets and around the wall,
I'll follow you wherever you are,
I'll follow you; you can't go far!

Phoebe Walker (11)
Cockfield Primary School

I Saw

I saw a twelve-hour clock, glistening, shiny and clean,
I saw a whiteboard, flexible and smooth,
I saw a green, long rubber, standing in my house,
I saw a puppy pencil case, perched on my bed,
I saw a thick hard book, juicy and squishy,
I saw a small water bottle, with lead right through it,
I saw a black school pencil, ticking away.

Nicole Walton (9)
Cockfield Primary School

A Scary Poem

Cackling on their brooms
Skeletons' bones chattering day and night
Vampires' fangs dripping red.
Mummies' bandages trailing along the floor,
None are as scary as our teachers.
Ha, ha, ha.

Cameron Watson (8)
Dean Bank School

A Scary Poem

S cary monsters under my bed
C reepy skeletons in the wardrobe
A wful scary they are, ghosts
R evolting blood dripping from the roof
Y ellow goo on the floor.

Issac Pearson (8)
Dean Bank School

A Scary Poem

Yellow eyes scare you,
'Boo,' the ghosts scream
Witches on their broomsticks
Flying through the night
Skeletons crack their bones.

Jacqueline Walker (8)
Dean Bank School

Hallowe'en

H eadless horseman chops off your head.
A t Hallowe'en the monsters rise from the dead.
L ocusts, rats in the cauldron.
L ittle spiders in the attic room.
O gres' clubs smack you down.
W itch's potion all thick and brown.
E vil Devil down in Hell.
E ating spiders, I don't feel well.
N asty singing of the witches, I would rather listen to a cow bell.

Amy Hopper (8)
Dean Bank School

A Scary Poem

S cary spiders
C reepy cats
A ngry anteaters
R isky potions
Y ucky food for tea.

James McCarthy (8)
Dean Bank School

Spooky Poem

Skeletons coming out of their graves
Witches laughing over their cauldrons
Big bat sucking blood
Time for Frankenstein
Have you seen Frankenstein?
Witches making spells
Big ogre scaring people
A ghost in the spooky house.

Christopher Palin (8)
Dean Bank School

A Scary Poem

S pooky skeleton
C ruel witches
A wful mummy
R ats stink
Y ellow ogres.

Jordan Walton (8)
Dean Bank School

A Scary Poem

G houls are scary
H aunted houses
O bnoxious ogres
U gly witches
L ittle cauldrons
S pitting snakes.

Brendan (8) & Jake Riseley (9)
Dean Bank School

A Scary Poem

S cary skeletons
C reepy spiders
A wful ogres
R otten mice
Y elling monster.

Lee Sheavils (8)
Dean Bank School

A Scary Poem

Skeleton bones clickety-clack.
Ghosts go *oooooooohhh*.
Witches screech.
Ogres roar
Yucky goo sloops.

Jessica Upton (8)
Dean Bank School

Untitled

Autumn years.
Autumn days.
When the world turns brown.
Leaves start to turn crisp.
Foggy morning.

Jacob Galpin (8)
Dean Bank School

A Scary Poem

W itches on broomsticks
I tchy backs of itchy rats
T urtle grease of meat and webs
C hunky rats
H ot cauldrons
E asing itching singers
S ingers having a heart attack on stage.

Matthew Limon (8)
Dean Bank School

A Scary Poem

S piders are scary with long pointy legs.
P ointy fangs are Dracula's best things.
O gre's club swings hard on your head.
O ver the fence there lies a bat waiting to get you.
K iller cats that are black, stay away from 'cause they'll get you.
Y ellow night, it's not a dream, watch out it might happen.

Rachael Farley (8)
Dean Bank School

A Scary Poem

T arantulas
R attlesnakes
A howl from a werewolf
N oises from Frankenstein's friends
S cary skeletons
Y elling in your attic
L oud bang from a cauldron
V ictims of the haunted house
A nt-eating maniacs
N ight-time comes, everyone scared
I n the haunted house someone dies
A zombie rising from the dead.

Nathan Wilson (8)
Dean Bank School

A Scary Poem

D ead bodies
E ating
V ampire's fangs
I tchy back
L icking blood.

Connor Pearson (8)
Dean Bank School

Spider

S limy snails with puppy dog's tails.
P umpkins and frogs on a plate with hogs.
I nside my body there are bones and groans.
D og's eyes and fifteen dead flies.
E yes and antelopes' horns with yellow and green thorns.
R ed icy blood dripping from the ceiling, blood from
   a dead man bleeding.

Caitlyn Atkinson (8)
Dean Bank School

A Scary Poem

S pooky vampires sucking blood
P elvises on a stick
'O rrible witches on broomsticks
O range ghosts behind the lamp posts
K iller Dracula in a coffin
Y ellow eyes glimmering.

Ewan Redhead (9)
Dean Bank School

The Feel Of Things

I like the feel of pizza
And the conkers so shiny.
Kicking a ball and pulling a door.
I like the horses when they clip-clop
And the feel of very cold bottles.

Liam Bailey (7)
East Stanley School

Senses

I like to look at butterflies when they land on a flower.
I like to touch wet, gooey, sticky sand.
I like to listen to dogs barking when they are angry.
I like to taste chocolate fudge cake when it sticks to my mouth.
I wish I was a bird so I could fly into the sky.

Rhiannon Quinn (7)
East Stanley School

Senses

I like to look at my mom's perfume because it's got flowers on it.
I like the touch of chicken feathers because they are smooth.
I like to listen to a bouncing ball because it goes *boing*.
I like to taste sweets because there are different kinds.
I wish I was Shevchenko to score lots of goals.

Ewan Taws (7)
East Stanley School

The Feel Of Things

I like the feel of newborn kittens.
The crackling of seaweed and soft sandy beaches.
I like the feel of wind in my ears.
The feel of icy snow.
And my baby brother's hair.
The smooth new sheets on my face.
And woolly new lambs.

Emily Chambers (7)
East Stanley School

Senses

I like to look at people walking about places.
I like to touch horse's hair.
I like to listen to metal clashing against wood.
I like to taste candy in my mouth getting munched up.
I wish I was a motorbike racer to be rich.

Joel Hall (8)
East Stanley School

Senses

I like the feel of tiny dogs, with their fluffy fur.
I like to look at horses running in a long race.
I like the sound of tigers roaring all the night.
I like to taste chocolate cake with cream inside it.
I wish I was flying on a unicorn.

Lucy Bates (7)
East Stanley School

Senses

I like the look of motor cars because they go really fast.
I like to look at fireworks because they are noisy.
I like the taste of chocolate fudge cake as it melts in my mouth.
I like the feel of ice cream.

Michael McNally (7)
East Stanley School

Senses

I like to look at dogs because they have nice fur.
I like to touch grass because it's nice and tickly.
I like to listen to birds singing all their nice songs.
I like to taste chocolate melting in my mouth.
I wish I was Frank Lampard because he gets lots of money.

Reece Jefferson (7)
East Stanley School

The Feel Of Things

I like the feel of carpet and the feel of brand new hay.
I like the feel of sand and a really slimy toy.
I like the feel of fur on dogs and the cold winter snow.
I like the feel of freshly cut grass and the feel of a fluffy teddy.

Ben Murphy (7)
East Stanley School

Senses

I like to look at zebras with three stripes.
I like to touch dogs, tingling through my fingers.
I like to listen to elephants running.
I like to taste sausages melting through my tongue.
I wish I was David Beckham scoring lots of goals.

Callum Boakes (7)
East Stanley School

Senses

I like to look at a fish swimming quietly in the water.
I like to touch a kitten's fur because it is smooth.
I like to touch a horse's hair because it is smooth.
I like to taste kiwi fruit because it is sour.

Stephen Chan (7)
East Stanley School

The Feel Of Things

I like the feel of wet sand on my toes.
I like the feel of little puppies.
I like the feel of the snow.
I like the rough leaves and the rough feel of wood.
I like the feel of soft carpets.

Summer Thompson (7)
East Stanley School

Senses

I like to listen to dogs barking in the backyard.
I like to touch brand new leather when I have new shoes.
I like to listen to the water tapping when I am in bed with the quilt

over me.

I like to taste custard swirling around my mouth.
I wish I was a bird flying so high in the sky.

Chloe Macallister (8)
East Stanley School

Senses

I like to look at the swishing water in the sea.
I like to touch horse's hooves because they are rough and smooth.
I like to listen to music because I love it so much.
I like to taste chocolate running down my throat.
I wish I was a Brat because they wear nice clothes.

Georgia Kent (7)
East Stanley School

Senses

I like to look at chocolate as it melts.
I like to touch teddy bears.
I like to listen to dogs when they bark.
I like to taste ice cream as it runs down my chin.
I wish I was a cat so I could eat more meat.

Sean Spinks (7)
East Stanley School

Senses

I like to look at dogs because I like to see them play.
I like to look at cars when they drive past.
I like to watch hair swishing.
I like to listen to birds singing because they wake me in the morning.
I like to taste chocolate melting in my mouth.
I like to touch the sofa because it is soft.

Emma Pickering (8)
East Stanley School

Senses

I like to look at fish as they splash about all day.
I like to look at people skipping.
I like the taste of fruit crushing in my mouth.
I like the feel of leather sofas.
I like to eat sweets because they are yummy.

Jade Bell (8)
East Stanley School

Senses

I like to look at cars because they go really fast.
I like to look at dinosaurs because I like to see their tails.
I like to touch sand because it is smooth.
I like to look at the lights on the Christmas tree.

Aiden Brown (7)
East Stanley School

The Feel Of Things

I like the feel of soft puppy's fur going down and down my hand
And smooth tingling grass.
I like the feel of rough towels against my body.
The chubby cheeks of my cousin.
I like the feel of sand tingling through my fingers.

Abigail Keall (7)
East Stanley School

Senses

I like to look at my sister's funny faces that make me laugh.
I like to touch the buttons on the computer because they are smooth.
I like to listen to music so I can dance.
I like to taste roast beef, scrummy in my tummy.
I wish I was a Brat, so I could shop by myself.

Kirsty Barnwell (8)
East Stanley School

The Feel Of Things

I like the feel of sand trickling through my toes
And my smooth rabbit's fur, thick under my fingers.
I like the feel of my sister's brown hair.
I like the feel of my soft skin.
But most of all I love the feel of my bed sheets.

Alicia Mallon (7)
East Stanley School

Senses

I like the look of apple juice because it is scrumptious,
I like the touch of brand new shiny shoes.
I like to listen to football because everybody says, 'Come on!'
I like the taste of icy cold yoghurt freezing from the fridge.
I wish I was Ronaldinho because he is the best player in the world.

Ryan Lister (7)
East Stanley School

Senses

I like the look of leopards with all the patterns.
I like the touch of brand new tables because they are smooth.
I like to listen to my music as it beats away.
I like the taste of chocolate melting in my mouth.
I wish I was Ronaldinho, the best footballer in the world.

Aaron Richardson (8)
East Stanley School

Animal Poem

A is for ant, strong and small
B is for bumblebee, they are not very tall!
C is for cat, whose eyes gleam at night
D is for dog, which can give a nasty bite.
E is for elephant, which sucks up water to soak
F is for frog, which goes, *'croak, croak'*
G is for gorilla, which is jet-black
H is for hamster, which is called Jack
I is for insect, which is small in size
J is for jaguar, which is extremely wise.
K is for kite, which zooms through the sky
L is for ladybird, which also can fly
M is for monkey, whose face is pale
N is for Nelly, my pet snail
O is for octopus, with long slimy legs
P is for pelican, which lays brown eggs
Q is for *'quack'* here comes the duck
R is for rabbit, which gives me good luck
S is for sharks, which have big jaws
T is for tigers, which have sharp claws
U is for unicorn, which drinks from the lake
V is for venom, which comes from a snake
W is for whale, which is big and chubby
X is for xxx (kisses) from my sloppy puppy
Y is for yak, which looks dark at night
Z is for zebra, which is black and white.

Eleanor Haswell (10)
East Stanley School

A To Z Of Footballers

A is for Adriano who is Brazilian
B is for Buffon who is Italian
C is for Cech who is a goalie
D is for Deco whose celebration is a roly-poly
E is for Eto'o who plays for Barcelona
F is for Ferreira who has a daughter called Mona
G is for Giggs who is thirty-two
H is for Henry who is much better than you
I is for Inzaghi who scored in the World Cup
J is for Jagielka who has got a lovely pup
K is for Kaka who is a midfielder
L is for Lampard who is a leader
M is for Martins who is Nigerian
N is for Nesta who is Italian
O is for Oleguer who is a defender
P is for Puyol who captains Barcelona as a defender
Q is for Quellini who is unknown
R is for Rooney who is one of the most known
S is for Scholes who is ginger
T is for Terry who is England's captain
U is for Unka who always likes
V is for Vidic who plays for Man U
W is for Walcott who's only scored two.
X is for Xain who is Spanish
Y is for Yorke who is really old
Z is for Zokora who plays for Tottenham and that is the end.

Ryan Bell (10)
East Stanley School

Amos

I have a new puppy and Amos is his name
He gets into a lot of trouble and mischief and always gets the blame.
I have to handle him with care and pat him when he is good
I see his water is always fresh and that he's got good food
I have to clean his ears and brush him every day.
And make sure his bed is clean and dry where he can go and lay
I try and be his best buddy
But it can be hard when he's naughty and muddy
I am trying to teach him how to heel and sit
Without him taking a puppy fit
It's good fun learning all the time
I am so glad Amos is all mine.

Dean Swinbank (10)
East Stanley School

Animals

Animals in every different place
Some are away
And some in your face

Some very small
Some so light in weight
They can crawl up the wall

Some are very fast
So nimble and thin
But their speed doesn't last

Animals can be guards
Or cute, fluffy pets
But pictures of them can be found on cards

Some are so creepy
They freak me out
Some hibernate when they are sleepy

Some in spring are born
Some have wings
And some dodge thorns.

Samantha Appleby (10)
East Stanley School

My Attic

In my attic there's a rotting sandwich
An old telescope all rusty and old
Also a clock ticking in the background
Old picture frames and ancient photos
Rotting sandwiches under the cupboard
Rats scurrying across the floor
Slime running down the concrete
An old Hallowe'en mask on the floor.
That's my attic.

James Blanchard (10)
East Stanley School

Winter Wonderland

Snowflakes falling all around
Snowmen melting on the ground
Children playing snowball fights
While darkness creeps upon the nights!

Christmas is on the way,
But before that is another day,
Christmas Eve is what we call it,
Children get excited for it!

Lights are lighting up the square,
And lights are blazing everywhere,
Twelve hours to go until Christmas Day,
And Santa Claus is on his way!

Children go upstairs to bed,
While magic dreams fill their head.
At 7.30 they run downstairs
To see if they've got rocking chairs!

They open presents all day long
And some boys have got King Kong.
There's just another 365 days to wait,
But poor Santa's just getting through the gate!

Hannah Emmerson (10)
East Stanley School

Spooky House

That spooky house, that spooky house,
I watch it from my bedroom window.
I watch it through the telescope.
The owner's name is old man Nevercrakers
Creepy man, my friend Chowder lost his new ball
Nevercracker came out and took Chowder's ball
He takes everything that lands on his lawn.
We never saw the ball again.

Ben Storey (9)
East Stanley School

Winter Fantasy

Snowflakes falling on my tongue,
Snowmen dancing in the sun.
Children run and laugh and play
What a wonderful winter fan-ta-say,
Putting up the Christmas tree
Lights are blaring back at me
Santa's sleigh bells on my roof
Put on my new pink jellies
Climb into bed, snuggle up tight
Up to my neck, I hear Santa in the night.
Six-thirty in the morning shoot downstairs
To see if Santa has left me some bears
Cookies are all gone, nothing left,
We thought that Santa had made a theft
Open my prezzies and guess what I find
A bone for my dog that he left underground
What a wonderful winter fantasy.

Jessica Bates (10)
East Stanley School

The Babysitter

It was clear from the moment
They walked out the door
That Tracey
Had never done this job before
Until they came home
She patiently
Sat on me,
My little brother
And the cat.

Dominic Cox (10)
East Stanley School

Fireworks!

Fireworks go off on Guy Fawkes Day.
When they go off they make a really loud sound,
When they go up in to the sky
They come in all different sizes and colours.

Shannon Gray (9)
East Stanley School

Fireworks!

Light the string,
Wait for a while,
Look in the air,
Then sparks will be there,
They light the sky,
They hurt your ears.
Watch yourself
If you get hit it will really, really hurt.

Dean Greaves (9)
East Stanley School

Lightning McQueen

I'm Lightning McQueen
I'm super fast,
I'm going to win,
Not come last,
Because I'm a blast.

Andrew Nealen (9)
East Stanley School

Shooting Rocket

What's that so way up high
Shining brightly in the sky?
Sparks are flying in your trail
Shooting faster than a whale
Bright colours come and go
Weee and off we gooo!

Molly Cruddas (9)
East Stanley School

The Liverpool Football Poem

Whistle goes, game flowing
Here comes Stevie G
Has a shot
The ball goes in and the Kop shouts, 'Goal.'

Here we go again
Agger bursting forward
Left foot, ball goes 65 mph
In the top corner

Here's Zenden, don't lose it son
Passes to Riise, tracer bullet,
Keeper misses, whoops.

Final whistle goes, Liverpool
Champions of Europe again, six times
Now must be a record, Steven Gerrard
Once again lifts the cup with pride.

Conrad Ashton (10)
Middlestone Moor Primary School

Love and Romance Poem

Love and romance is pink like the sunset.
It tastes like chocolate pudding with
Pink, creamy custard.
It smells like scented oils.
It looks like cupid with a bow and arrow.
It sounds like ping when the arrow hits
The humans.
It feels like fur from a cuddly bear.

Jade Lawlor (10)
Middlestone Moor Primary School

The Nonsense Poem

I'm that book on the shelf
If you read me you'll have wealth
I smell like a dog
My title is Fog
I'm in a bookcase
I'm last place
In the book race
My pace is faster
Than a suitcase
I was written in by a feather
And my second name is Heather.

Jamie Longthorne (10)
Middlestone Moor Primary School

Hate Poem

Hate is grey like a stormy day.
It tastes like the bitterness of sick.
It looks like a dark shadow that is always there.
It smells like a damp, dusty house.
It sounds like a girl screaming and crying.
It feels like cold baked beans.

Katie O'Rourke (10)
Middlestone Moor Primary School

We All Love Happiness

Happiness is green like Stamford Bridge.
It tastes like chocolate cake.
It smells like a heart full of love.
It sounds like a Chelsea match.
It feels like a nice, soft bed.

Liam Daglish (10)
Middlestone Moor Primary School

Anger

Anger is like a dark misty cloud.
It looks like a roaring fire.
It sounds like people screaming at each other.
It tastes like lumpy, cold rice pudding.
It feels like people poking needles in your back.
It smells like damp, wet fog.

Bethany Gulliver (10)
Middlestone Moor Primary School

Happiness

Happiness is gold like glowing stars.
It tastes like treacle tart with dripping vanilla ice cream.
It smells like my mam's chicken dinner.
It looks like a Chelsea player scoring a goal.
It feels like Chelsea winning the Premiership.

Alexander Tonge (10)
Middlestone Moor Primary School

The Bully

Malcolm Mully,
Was a big bully.
He bullied poor Sally-Jane.
She told him she was going to tell if he
Did it again.
So what did he do?
The silly old fool
Bullied Sally again
She reported him to a teacher
And Sally never had a problem
Ever again.

So if it happens to you
You know what to do
Tell a teacher, adult or friend
And your problem will end.

Zoe Hauxwell (11)
Middlestone Moor Primary School

England Take The Aussies

England win the toss
The Aussies will show them who is boss
Strauss takes on Brett Lee
He hits the ball to the sea
England at one hundred and twelve for five
Vaughan goes for a dive
Umpire says, 'Out'
Gillespie needs some stout
Freddie comes in, he is not going to lack
Warney breaks his back
They all go round the bend
And that is the end.

Kieran Kyle (10)
Middlestone Moor Primary School

Happiness Poem

Happiness is pink like the early morning sky.
It tastes like melted white chocolate.
It smells like a bunch of multicoloured flowers.
It looks like a field of baby animals.
It sounds like sweet singing from a children's choir.
It feels like a fresh plate of buttery biscuits.

Leanne Pearson (10)
Middlestone Moor Primary School

Loneliness

Loneliness is grey like a haunted house.
It tastes like sour juice crawling down my throat.
It smells like a muddy surface at
St James' Park after a football match.
It looks like a never-ending back alley.
It sounds like people's voices echoing.
It feels like the walls are closing in on me.

Alex Close (10)
Middlestone Moor Primary School

Pain

Pain is red like the flames of fire.
Pain tastes like the sourest sweet in the world.
Pain smells like a breath of fresh air.
Pain sounds like plodding footsteps.
Pain feels like the Devil poking you with his fork.

Sarah Barnes (11)
Middlestone Moor Primary School

Enjoyment Poem

Enjoyment is yellow like the sun.
It tastes like ice lollies melting in your mouth.
It smells like the sea.
It looks like a bird swirling towards you.
It sounds like waves crashing amongst you.
It feels like the sun beaming on you.

Jordan Palmer (11)
Middlestone Moor Primary School

The Playground

Children running
People falling
Balls flying
People crying
Rackets flying
Cricket arguing
Noses bleeding
Teachers weeping
Bells ringing
Doors clashing.

James Foreman (10)
Middlestone Moor Primary School

Fear

Fear is like a black stormy night.
It tastes like you've just been sick.
It smells like rotten eggs.
It looks like a pile of rubbish.
It sounds like you can hear noises outside of your house.
It feels like someone peeping out of something.

Hannah Gulliver (10)
Middlestone Moor Primary School

Pup

I awake
Look for private place in the house
Find one at last
Sleep
I awake
I look for private place in the house
I find one straight away this time
Right in front of the TV
Sleep
I awake
Drink
Eat
I find a different one this time
In my owner's lap
Sleep.

Stacey Doughty (10)
Middlestone Moor Primary School

Happiness United

Happiness is black and white like Newcastle United.
It tastes like Newcastle's finest tea.
It sounds like a football ground.
It feels like Newcastle winning the Premiership.

Marcus Brownless (10)
Middlestone Moor Primary School

Untitled

Happiness is yellow like the brightest Spanish sun.
It tastes like the ripest banana.
It smells like the nicest perfume.
It looks like a crystal-blue sea.
It sounds like the calmest music.
It feels like the softest skin.

Ryan Whitehead (10)
Middlestone Moor Primary School

My Emotions

Happiness is the colours of a rainbow.
It tastes like warm coffee on a cold, windy day.
It smells like a bed of roses.
It looks like open green fields.
It sounds like birds singing in the tree tops.
It feels like being loved.

Sad is red like the darkest blood.
It tastes like frozen chips.
It smells like salty water.
It looks like falling down an elevator.
It sounds like a slow heartbeat.
It feels like being alone.

Love is white like a small fluffy cloud.
It tastes like hot chocolate.
It smells like people cooking.
It looks like the sun rising in the early morning.
It sounds like water running down a stream.
It feels like when you get in a lovely warm bath.

Chloe Smith (10)
Middlestone Moor Primary School

Love

Love is the colour pink.
It tastes like a family Christmas dinner.
It smells like a roast dinner.
It looks like a baby laughing.
It sounds like my family and opening presents.
It feels like a heart beating.

Kelly Cooney (10)
Middlestone Moor Primary School

Happiness Is . . .

Happiness is being cool.
Happiness is going on holiday.
Happiness is playing on Habbo.
Happiness is going boxing.
Happiness is slipping on ice.
Happiness is going swimming.
Happiness is getting toys.
Happiness is playing tig.
Happiness is shooting rats.
Happiness is being with my dad.
Happiness is having a birthday.
Happiness is sleeping.
Happiness is getting credits on Habbo.
Happiness is going to New York.
Happiness is daydreaming.
Happiness is going to Jenny's for tea.
Happiness is eating food.
Happiness is looking at my fish.
Happiness is searching the web.
Happiness is going to the pub.
Happiness is getting a week off school.
happiness is cooking a burger.
Happiness is money $$$.

J J Adair (8)
Mowden Junior School

Friends Are . . .

Friends are honest and truthful,
Friends never leave you out,
Friends share their cookies,
Friends are playful,
Friends invite you to their house.
Friends care for you if you get hurt,
Friends won't let your team down,
Friends are helpful,
Friends keep you happy,
Friends are funny and fun,
Friends get you presents from their holiday,
Friends will cheer you up on sports day,
Friends won't hurt you,
Friends email you,
Friends and you have sleepovers,
Friends are friends.

Eleanor Andrews (9)
Mowden Junior School

The Happiness Poem

Happiness is when I go to people's parties and get sweets there!
Happiness is when I spend time with my family and play games
with them.
Happiness is when I go to the park with my mum and dad
and my little sister!
Happiness is when I go on holiday and I have an incredible time!
Happiness is when I get presents.

Olivia Hugill (8)
Mowden Junior School

A List Poem

Happiness is an ear-piercing alarm.
Happiness is fun and games and always full of excitement.
Happiness is the sun's bright rays beaming down on us.
Happiness is a toy you can't stop playing with even if you're gloomy.
Happiness is going to a lovely forest and exploring new things.
Happiness is a holiday full of joy and love.
Happiness is a new friend to play with.
Happiness is someone saying jokes that make you laugh.
Happiness is reading an adventurous story.
Happiness is a faraway island I can never reach.
Happiness is when I get post delivered to me.
Happiness is when I get presents.
Happiness is when I get better from being sick.
Happiness is a merit on my card.
Happiness is a second passing by.

Richard Smith (8)
Mowden Junior School

Happiness

Happiness is a brand new football kit.
Happiness is when I finish an enjoyable book!
Happiness is when England win the World Cup.
Happiness is when I stroke my rabbit!

Jack Cooper (8)
Mowden Junior School

Jump Or Jiggle

Butterflies flutter
Chinchillas mutter,

Hyenas laugh
Rhinoceroses bath,

Elephants squirt
Tigers hurt,

Shrews creep
Weasels peep,

Pigs trot
Hares hop,

Pufferfish pop
Frogs plop,

Bugs jump
Camels have a hump,

Seals slide
Swans glide.

Tyler Skelton (8)
Mowden Junior School

Jump Or Jiggle

Fish glide,
Frogs hide.

Seagulls glide,
Sea snails slide.

Butterflies flutter,
Mice scutter.

Pigs walk,
Planktons stalk.

Dogs hound,
Cats pound.

Pufferfish pop,
Hens eat crop.

Horses clop,
Bunnies hop!

Bugs wiggle,
Salamanders jiggle.

Lions stalk,
I walk.

Caterpillars hump,
Moles thump.

Hyenas laugh,
Giraffes bath.

Jack Norcup (8)
Mowden Junior School

Happiness Is . . .

Happiness is my warm puppy.
Happiness is a nice cool drink.
Happiness is when Liverpool win the match.
Happiness is a big hug off my mum.
Happiness is a pair of new boots.
Happiness is a boiling hot chocolate.
Happiness is a big kiss off my dad.
Happiness is a Christmas dinner.
Happiness is when I go horse riding.
Happiness is when I go swimming.
Happiness is reading a fantastic book.
Happiness is when I go trick or treating.
Happiness is when me and my mum went to see the Queen.
Happiness is when Abi and Gary and Laura play with me.
Happiness is when I meet new friends.
Happiness is when I get rewards.
Happiness is when I go to Lightwater Valley.
Happiness is when I go to bed.

Caitlin Stabler (8)
Mowden Junior School

Happiness Is . . .

Happiness is getting presents.
Happiness is having pets.
Happiness is Xmas dinner.
Happiness is having fun.
Happiness is England winning a match.
Happiness is playing in the snow.
Happiness is buying a new house.
Happiness is having tea.
Happiness is playing sports.
Happiness is going fishing.
Happiness is doing art.
Happiness is having birthdays.

Jonathon Dent (8)
Mowden Junior School

Happiness

Happiness is when I got a new mum and dad.
Happiness is when I got an England duvet cover.
Happiness is when I got a nice grandma.
Happiness is when I got some nice treats on the fantastic weekend
off school.

James Marshall (8)
Mowden Junior School

Happiness

Happiness is a cool refreshing drink after football!
Happiness is a goal when I play football!
Happiness is when I have a nice family holiday!
Happiness is when I play in the park after a refreshing sweet!
Happiness is a nice chicken and a curry!
Happiness is a good football match at Newcastle!

Daniel Crane (8)
Mowden Junior School

Happiness

Happiness is when I come home from holiday and I'm really excited
to see my friends and family.
Happiness is a warm cuddle with my mum.
Happiness is when my dad annoys me!
Happiness is when I see my grandmas and grandads and we play
Fascinating games.
Happiness is when I have a gorgeous and lovely Christmas dinner
with my grandmas and grandads.
Happiness is when I play on the swings and see-saws
at the South Park.
Happiness is when I've had a party and when my friends have a party.
Happiness is when my mum pulls funny faces.
Happiness is a bundle of laughter!
Happiness is when I draw a picture of myself.
Happiness is when my friends are honest and truthful with me
and don't break promises.

Hollie Sanderson (8)
Mowden Junior School

Happiness

Happiness is a big hug with my rabbit.
Happiness is a nice Christmas dinner.
Happiness is a nice hot chocolate.
Happiness is spending time with my mum and dad and Jonathan.
Happiness is going round people's homes to trick or treat.
Happiness is a time with my best friends.
Happiness is a time to go on a roller coaster.
Happiness is a time to go and see my grandma's dog, Kim.
Happiness is a nice hug with my mum and dad.
Happiness is a nice chocolate cake.

Emily Carroll (8)
Mowden Junior School

Animal Alphabet Poem

Action ants ate apples sweetly.
Brilliant bats bring baseball bats.
Camping cat camps crazily.
Diving dolphin dives dramatically.
Exercising elephant entertains especially.
Funny fish fantastically farms.
Grandma giraffe grants green grapes.
Hairy hippopotamus hits hens hard.
Intelligent iguana interferes and ignores.

Ben McMain (9)
Mowden Junior School

Happiness Is . . .

Happiness is a refreshing drink.
Happiness is a huge hug.
Happiness is going swimming.
Happiness is a great big bar of chocolate.
Happiness is winning the Cup Final 2006.
Happiness is spending time with your family.
Happiness is finishing a great big piece of art.
Happiness is a friend.

David Wilcock (9)
Mowden Junior School

Jump Or Jiggle

Butterflies flutter,
Bears mutter.

Wolves howl,
Lions growl.

Crickets jump,
Caterpillars hump.

Woodpeckers tap,
Birds flap.

Monkeys grin,
Whales swim.

Josh O'Brien (8)
Mowden Junior School

Happiness Is . . .

Happiness is finding a big fat conker on the soft ground.
Happiness is finishing a piece of brilliant work.
Happiness is a gorgeous plate of fish and chips.
Happiness is a brand new toy.
Happiness is making great friends.
Happiness is scoring a fantastic goal.
Happiness is reading a fascinating book.
Happiness is spending time with my family when we are doing
something special.
Happiness is having a fun day at school.
Happiness is having a laugh with my friends.

Thomas Richard Rayner (8)
Mowden Junior School

Happiness

Happiness is love and care.
Happiness is a new baby child.
Happiness is getting a gold medal
Happiness is going swimming on a scorching hot day.
Happiness is playing cricket with Daddy.
Happiness is reading a story with Mummy.
Happiness is watching nature in autumn.
Happiness is a new piece of gorgeous clothing.
Happiness is a new bouncy ball.
Happiness is winning a game of chess.
Happiness is playing a fabulous game with Lucy.
Happiness is opening an elegant present.
Happiness is chilly winter, cool spring, warm summer
                              and dusky autumn.

Eleanor Bairstow (8)
Mowden Junior School

Happiness

Happiness is watching scary films.
Happiness is winning an obstacle race.
Happiness is when the loud fire alarm goes off.
Happiness is when I get sent for a big sticker.
Happiness is getting delicious sweets.
Happiness is having a fun sleepover.
Happiness is making a pretty picture.

Hayley Howard   (9)
Mowden Junior School

My Funny Animal Poem

Butterflies flutter,
Chimpanzees mutter,

Camels hump,
Giraffes bump,

Cats explore,
Alligators adore,

Lions creep,
Joeys sleep,

Tigers doze,
Frogs pose,

Meerkats hop,
Bugs pop,

Wolves prowl,
Dogs howl,

Bears drizzle
Hyenas grizzle,

Birds fly,
Horses lie,

Pigs hide,
Owls glide,

Mice nibble,
Parrots giggle,

Goats boast,
Iguanas post,

Elephants are fat,
Hippos bat.

Georgia Broadbent (9)
Mowden Junior School

Jump Or Jiggle

Butterflies flutter
Bears mutter

Fish plop
Horses clop

Kangaroos jump
Camels hump

Salamanders slither
Polar bears shiver

Hyenas laugh
Seals are tough

Frogs hop
Jellyfish plop

Dogs play
Sheep like hay.

Jake Powely (8)
Mowden Junior School

A List Poem

Friends are kind and helpful,
Friends are a nice soft toy,
Friends are a bowl of yummy treats,
Friends are bringing lots of sweets,
Friends are filled with fashion,
Friends are . . .

Holly Marks (8)
Mowden Junior School

Animals!

Gators snap,
Birds flap!

Cheetahs pounce,
Kangaroos bounce,

Swans glide,
Chameleons hide,

Cats creep,
Deer leap,

Fireflies dance,
Peacocks prance,

Lionesses growl,
Kittens prowl,

Cats stalk,
But I
Walk!

Thomas Peter William McDonald (8)
Mowden Junior School

Jump Or Jiggle

Puppies play
Horses neigh

Worms wiggle
Bugs jiggle

Rabbits hop
Walruses flop

Crickets crunch
Mice munch

Snakes slide
Seagulls glide.

Emma McGarrell (8)
Mowden Junior School

List Poem

Family is kind when you're down,
Family is like your very best friend,
Family is playing a family game,
Family is having a fun and fantastic time on holiday,
Family is your life and death,
Family is . . .

Luke Hutchinson (8)
Mowden Junior School

Animal Alphabet Poem

Angry antelope ate ants.
Bare bear bathes beautifully.
Cute chimp climbs chimneys.
Dancing deer dances all night.
Exercising earwig exercises elegantly.
Fat frog fries food.
Gay goose gallops gaily.

Lucy Hodgson (8)
Mowden Junior School

Animal Alphabet Poem

Alligators attack animals,
Baboons have blue bums,
Cats catch crabs,
Dolphins do the dance at sea,
Elephants explain their big ears,
Fish cuddle the fancy frogs,
Goats go to gossip in their home,
Hyenas howl on holiday,
Insects walk along the igloo and insects' path,
Jaguars jump in Japan,
Kangaroos kick to do the conga,
Lions leap and laze around all day,
Monkeys munch on marzipan.

Laura Whitehouse (9)
Mowden Junior School

Animal Movement

Lizards lick
Monkeys pick

Lions growl
Hyenas howl

Spiders spin
Cheetahs win

Rabbits hop
Horses clop

Mice creep
Cats weep

Chameleons hide
Seagulls glide.

Kieran Joel Harman Spencer (9)
Mowden Junior School

A Pet Is . . .

A pet is a friendly creature
A pet is cunning
A pet is a cuddly thing
My pet always gets in a muddle
So beware she doesn't nibble
Don't hurt it and don't be scared.

Bethany John (8)
Mowden Junior School

A List Poem

Friends are sweet, soft kittens,
Friends are warm, fluffy mittens,
Friends are bowls full of sweets,
Friends are bringing scrummy treats,
Friends are full of fun fashion,
Friends are sparkling with passion,
Friend are making me laugh,
Friends are starting to barf,
Friends are . . .

Sophie Naisbitt (8)
Mowden Junior School

Animal Poem

Monkeys swing
Bats dangle

Kangaroos hop
Rabbits prance

Lions creep
Frogs jiggle

Horses clop
I walk.

Chris Vardy (8)
Mowden Junior School

Animal Alphabet Poem

Ants skate up and down and round and round, here and there,
Stealing food and stuff.
Bats, they come out at night, they fly here and there,
You can't see them.
Cats are good and cute, they play with a ball madly.
Adders are mean, they spit and hiss and bite and fight.

Callam Luke Jobling (8)
Mowden Junior School

Family Are . . .

Family is kind and helpful.
Family is having fun and games with family.
Family is a cute, cuddly family dog.
Family is kind cousins.
Grandmas are kind and if you don't win a race they say,
                                          'Doesn't matter.'

Callum Gault (8)
Mowden Junior School

Animal Alphabet Poem

Alligators attack when other animals come into their territory.
Baboons have blue bottoms.
Cats creep at night and creep during the day.
Dolphins do show dancing.
Elephants lay enormous eggs.
Fish feed on flaky food.
Goats giggle when they go to Great Britain.
Hyenas howl on horrible holidays.
Insects walk along the insecty path.
Jaguars jiggle when they jump to the music.
Kangaroos kick to the conga.
Lions leap and lay all day.
Monkeys munch on mangoes.

Ellie Louise Lawson (8)
Mowden Junior School

ABC Animal Poem

Ants like to munch before eating their lunch.
Butterflies like to swoop while flying too low.
Cats like to pounce while catching a mouse.
Dogs like to doze while flapping their ears.
Elephants like to explain to the little kangaroos.
Frogs like to hop in the clear blue pond.
Giraffes like to stretch right up to the stars.
Horses like to be a wobbling rodeo.
Iguanas identify their mothers.

Michael John English (8)
Mowden Junior School

Pets Are . . .

Pets are so crazy and kind.
Pets are cute and cuddly puppies.
Pets are having a puppy.
Pets are my pet guinea pig
Pets can play all day
Pets like to explore outside.

Emma Raine (8)
Mowden Junior School

Jump Or Jiggle

Horses neigh
Dogs play.

Frogs jump
Camels bump.

Worms wiggle
Bags jiggle.

Mice creep
Deer leap.

Lions stalk
But we walk.

Rabbits hop
But we walk.

Tom O'Brien (8)
Mowden Junior School

Animal Alphabet Poem

Armadillos are arrogant,
Bears become beastly and brutish,
Cats are callous and cruel,
Dogs demand delicious things,
Elephants are elegant,
Frogs are frightened and ferocious,
Goats giggle and gas,
Horses hop and clop,
Iguana identified his grandpa,
Jaguar jumps on his prey,
Kangaroo kisses baby kangaroo,
Lion limps back to the pride,
Magpie steals a necklace from the Queen,
Newt knits his coat,
Octopus orders his crown,
Panther pounces on his prey,
Quail gives the class a quiz,
Reindeer ripples the water,
Snake slithers silently through the scorching sand,
Tiger tickles Thomas the tiger.

John Lorimer (8)
Mowden Junior School

Animal Alphabet Poem

Alligators absolutely love to eat apples,
Butterflies fly high in the big blue sky,
Cats love to play with cute, cuddly toys,
Dolphins live in the deep blue sea,
Elephants are nearly extinct from the wild,
Frogs frantically fly and jump everywhere,
Goats graze slowly on the green, green grass,
Horses hiss when they go on holiday,
Iguanas love to eat incy wincy insects,
Jaguars jump and jiggle and juggle at the same time,
Kangaroos kick conkers all over Australia,
Lions lick sticky leftover lollies,
Monkey Molly munches and mutters to mummy monkey,
Newts niggle and jiggle and pick their noses all day.

Hannah Caitlin Alderson (9)
Mowden Junior School

Jump Or Jiggle

Butterflies flutter
Bears mutter

Salamanders slither
Arctic birds shiver

Fleas hop
Donkeys clop

Penguins slide
Seagulls glide

Snakes jiggle
Worms wiggle.

Thomas William Armstrong (8)
Mowden Junior School

Animals!

Swans glide,
Fish hide,

Deer jump,
Flies dive in the dump,

Caterpillars eat,
Butterflies meet,

Birds squawk,
Pigs turn into yummy pork.

Patrick Burney (8)
Mowden Junior School

An Alphabet Animal Poem

Angry ape ate bananas.
Brave bear battles on.
Crazy cat catches a crab.
Dancing duck dances all night.
Enormous elephant catches a bird.
Fat fish flaps its flippers.
Gorgeous giraffes grapple grapes.
Helpful hippos hang around.
Interesting iguana impresses the people.
Jumping Joey jumps happily.
Kicking kangaroo hops beautifully.
Lonely lion roars loudly.
Mickey Mouse mooches around.
Noisy narwhales play games.
Okay ostrich wiggles and is friendly to everyone in town.
Playing in the sea and having fun, penguins.
Quails quietly quench their thirst.
Rhinos race against the wind.
Slippery snake slithers along.
Turtles toss and turn in the sand.
Unicorns are magical.
Victory for the snarling vixen.
Whale snuffles loudly.
X-rays are used for the animals.
Yawning yak running in fields.
Zoo animals are looked after and kept safe.

Kathryn Haynes (8)
Mowden Junior School

Deep In The Forest

Deep in the forest
Where spongy, mossy ground lies.
You can hear cracking of fallen twigs on
The damp fungal ground underfoot.
The blazing sun shining through the grey blanket of mist,
Through the canopy tree tops like an eagle's eye.
The smell of dragon's breath over the trickling rough water.
Whilst the branches are shaking hands with the wind
Through the bright clean sky.
With red russet and bright green leaves
The velvet green moss on the dampened forest floor
When the wind is howling like an agitated wolf.

Joshua Bynoe (10)
Mowden Junior School

In The Water

In the water.
Waves of clashing lions
Clawing their way through the water.
Crashing giants, clashing waves,
Giants and lions demolishing each other.
The giant waves lost.

In the water.
Back for their revenge.
The four giants want their justice,
Slaying back the water.

Lions awake from their slumber
They coil in attack positions,
Giants are splashing through,
The fight is over
No one has won,
So no one rules the reservoir anymore.

Alex Miller (10)
Mowden Junior School

Deep In The Forest

Deep in the forest where the moss lies,
It's as green as a carpet.
The sun wakes up and looks so pretty,
It looks as golden as my happy face.
As you walk through the forest you can hear,
The sound of the leaves crunching under your feet.
The tall trees chattering in the wind,
Drop their golden and russet leaves as autumn approaches.
The damp smell of moss spreads through the forest.

Crystelle Challands (11)
Mowden Junior School

Autumn

Autumn quickly overtakes the summer
The leaves dance like ballerinas
The mist covers the sky like snakes slithering
Leaves parachuting across the sky.

Autumn standing on leaves making
Them crunch and snap.
The beautiful colours of bronze, gold and
Copper, carpeting the floor,
The hedgerows full of scarlet, maroon and
Purple berries attracting their prey.

Selina Todd (10)
Mowden Junior School

Leaves

On a bright sunny day,
The leaf appears.
It sways in the fresh, cold breeze,
And soon after it makes new friends,
The bright pink blossoms,
Like priceless crystals.
Together they flutter and play . . .
But as the years go by,
The sycamores fall,
The leaves know the time has come.
They dance and prance to the crispy ground,
All the way to their deathbed.
The cold white blanket covers them,
To keep them safe from harm,
And to keep them snug.
Waiting to dance again,
In paradise . . .

Katherine Louise Armstrong (10)
Mowden Junior School

Autumn

The leaves get ready,
And parachute down,
They land beneath your feet.
To and fro,
The trees do swing,
Bringing the leaves to the ground.
The mist comes over,
And keeps them warm and snug.
When the sun comes up,
It lifts the cream mist,
And then throws it in the sky.
The sun still rises and sees the leaves,
Dancing and twirling around.
When he dips the leaves start crackling,
People watch as they die.
Then it stops leaping and dancing about,
As the winter takes over.

Samuel Howard (10)
Mowden Junior School

Autumn

Autumn creeps through the silent wood
Shaking hands with the trees.
He rips the leaves
Throws them away
Then moves on.

Autumn moves like a silent bird
Flying soft and smoothly.
He swifts and turns
Flies up and down
Creating a stiff morning breeze.

Autumn has finished
He waves goodbye to the world.
He welcomes winter
Lies down to sleep
Until next year.

Humza Malik (10)
Mowden Junior School

Kielder Forest

In the middle of the forest, where it's dark,
The sun tries to break through the trees' branches.
I stand listening to the birds singing and the crickets rubbing their
legs together.

The mossy ground soaks up water like a sponge,
The wind sounds like people talking faintly.
The tall trees stand, swaying from side to side,
I can see fungi for miles and miles,
I can see deer-prints engraved in the mud
I can smell the plants in the air,
In the forest.

Hannah Jenkinson (10)
Mowden Junior School

The Forest

Deep in the forest
The strong smell of rotting fungi fills the air,
The spongy like moss spreads across the ground like
a newly laid carpet.
The sun's rays break through the trees like a golden rainbow,
The freshly broken acorns turn golden-brown in the sun,
The trees whine like a hungry dog,
The dry mud sets like a freshly baked chocolate cake,
The clouds float overhead as fluffy as candyfloss.
A sudden downpour starts,
Breaking the peace,
Lightning thunders down from the rapidly blackening sky,
The wind rages, like a howling wolf!
Rain comes down like giants' tears,
The sun disappears.

Matthew Crane (11)
Mowden Junior School

Kielder Forest

In the heart of the forest
Where the floor is a carpet of damp green moss
The sun breaks through the gaps in the clouds
A happy ray of sunshine breaks free
The lake is as calm as a contented baby
Still and peaceful
The fine grey mist emerges on the horizon
As it emerges the branches shake hands with the wind
You can hear the crunching of the leaves
The tweeting of the birds
You can see the eager grey squirrel
Scurrying along the damp forest floor
The wind blows against my cheeks
Making them go the colour of cherries
The sun goes down
Down from where it first came up
Over Kielder Forest.

Fiona Lupton (10)
Mowden Junior School

Autumn

Autumn crept,
Through the maze of houses,
Into the whispering wood,
Trying his hardest not to wake,
The children in their sleep.
The trees' hair blew all over,
As they danced the night away,
Their golden leaves falling, twirling, twisting,
Playing on the floor.
The wind whistled and howled,
As the party grew larger and larger,
The trees stripped bare,
The muddy floor covered in a golden carpet.
Suddenly the weather cooled,
Frost appeared on the bare trees,
'Goodbye' Autumn said.
And snuggled into his soft, warm bed.

Elizabeth Oliver (11)
Mowden Junior School

Autumn

Autumn tiptoes,
On his soft paws,
Through the whispering wood,
Like a vain cat
He paws at the trees,
Knocking resting conkers
Out of their soft sleeping bags.

Autumn dances,
On its hind legs
Through his new world,
Like a ballerina
Dancing around the trees,
Leaves twirling, whirling in the air
Floating like clouds.

Autumn leaps
On all fours
Through his new world,
Like a train
He puffs out air,
Making a strong gust of wind,
Trees shaking, full of fright.

Autumn tiptoes,
On his soft paws
Back from his new world,
Like a vain cat
Waving goodbye to his creations,
Now it's time for Autumn to sleep
For Winter's alive once more . . .

Hannah Dennis (11)
Mowden Junior School

Autumn

Autumn takes over from summer,
The leaves are ballet dancers prancing and dancing around.

The moss is a smooth, damp carpet on the forest floor.
The leaves fall from the sky as they twirl.

The trees are soldiers waiting for instructions as they
Lose their protective clothing.

The colourful berries on the bush brighten up the whole forest.

But it will fade away.
Winter will come.

Until next year,
It will come again.

Jordan Moohan (11)
Mowden Junior School

Autumn

Autumn prowls through the night.
Watching for trees to strip bare of their leaves.
Leaves falling, dancing, spinning around.
Rain like shattered glass pours down onto the hard floor,
Autumn then creeps around for something to do.
But what?

Autumn and her lips open wide and a gust of wind blows around.
The morning rises, autumn calms down,
She looks for something to strip,
Leaves to rip off,
A branch, a twig to snap.

The sun starts to come out,
Autumn is relieved that her job is finally over,
But what can she do now?
Winter is taking over rapidly,
It rains more, autumn needs to work harder,
What more can she do?

The bonfires stop cracking and spitting onto the golden-leaved floor.
Autumn has lost her strength.
Autumn is going, fading away.
Gone.
Winter has taken over!

Hayley Soanes (11)
Mowden Junior School

Autumn

Autumn marched,
Through the deserted, howling forest.
Scaring animals and birds in their burrows.
Knocking conkers out of their warm, cosy beds.
Splashing and sprinkling a lovely crimson paint,
With his icy breath he blows wind,
Which makes the leaves fall like dancing ballerinas.
Stealing them from the trees.
Autumn, a giant barging down upon everything,
Stomping along the white frosty riverbank.
As he moves to his next place to destroy!

Jonathan O'Neill (10)
Mowden Junior School

The Mossy Forest

Down in the forest,
Where tall trees sway in the wind,
The mist is like a sheet of glass,
As the trees groan and yawn as they wake up.
The moss on the ground is as bouncy as a trampoline,
The bird fluttering in the sky.

Trees so tall they touch the bright sun,
The fallen trees groan with pain.
When you walk into the forest,
You have entered another world.
The fungi in a huddle,
Telling their daily news.

Michael Bell (10)
Mowden Junior School

The Forest

As the sun breaks through the branches,
The crackling of leaves I can hear,
Bouncing as I walk on the green carpet of moss.
But then the sun goes and the wind comes,
The branches of the trees shake hands with the wind,
The mist follows, covering the ground, like a white blanket.
Then the golden sun returns,
Lifting the mist with his hand-like rays,
The sound of flowing water, I can hear,
As if a tap has been left running.
I can feel the damp leaves,
The hard, wrinkly bark,
The forest all peaceful as I leave.

Danielle Wright (11)
Mowden Junior School

Kielder Forest

Deep in the forest
Fungi lies across the floor which is
A cushion-like carpet made out of green moss
I hear twigs snapping, leaves rustling.
I can see creatures rushing to their homes.
Trees shaking hands with the wind,
Noisy planes bending, twisting, turning in the sky, disturbing
                                                    nature's peace
The golden sun cracks through the trees.
Sending golden spears of light into the tree trunks
                                and onto the ground.
Footprints in the mud from people walking through the forest.
The sky like a blue carpet covering the forest above.

Katie Finch (10)
Mowden Junior School

Autumn Memories

Autumn creeps silently sending summer to its grave,
Marshmallow mist burning in the bonfires,
Leaves changing outfits to a jester,
Also floating in the air like a genie mat,
Sycamore seed swirling so soft, so silent,
Onto a carpet of leaves.
Catherine wheels playing like little girls,
Swirling in circles again and again.
The conkers getting snug in their little duvet,
The winter comes and attacks
Autumn loses and slowly walks away.

Robyn Colling (10)
Mowden Junior School

Autumn

Autumn waves goodbye to summer,
Locking the sun behind the clouds,
The sun lets off its last droplets of golden warmth,
Then that's it for the year.

Autumn creeps,
Through the whispering wood,
Sneaking around the trees,
Like a hunting fox.

Autumn sneezes,
Making the leaves prance and dance,
Leaves changing colour like chameleons,
Rusty red, burnt brown, golden yellow,
A rainbow-coloured carpet to walk upon.

Autumn tiptoes,
Knocking down all the acorns from the trees
Animals saving food for spring,
Getting ready to be warm and cosy,
And enjoy a spring feast.

Autumn now shakes hands with winter,
In a friendly kind of way,
Now it is winter's turn to do all of the work,
Autumn is now in bed for a year.

Lauren Jordinson (10)
Mowden Junior School

Autumn!

Autumn rushes from town to town,
Grabbing the leaves and leaving the trees bare.
Golds, bronzes and coppers,
Stripped and left on the floor,
To be crushed by feet and left to blow away.

He rushes through the forests,
He skims over the waters,
Like a speedboat racing.
Nipping the fungi he moves on.
Making everything frosty.

Leaves dance and prance from the trees,
Like a ballerina in her show.
Leaving the trees bare and taking the leaves with him,
To his world of frost!

Spreading over the grass,
Making it white like a crystal,
Conkers snuggled up in their tent,
Fast asleep till they drop to the floor.

Mist, mist as grey as smoke spreading through the
Sky and looking down on the world,
Making it cold and unfriendly.
Marking its territory.

Leaves in piles ready to be burnt,
The bonfire like the blinding sun hugging the sky.
Higher and higher the flames climb up,
Killing the frost with its blinding scarlet colour.

Winter is coming to take over,
To cover the forest and treetops,
With a white fluffy blanket,
Autumn is dying out!

Chloe Newsome (10)
Mowden Junior School

Autumn

Autumn creeps,
Through the wood crunching leaves and twigs,
Autumn observes leaves like ballerinas dancing to the floor,
Autumn prowls,
Past birds eating bright red berries,
Autumn smells the smoke,
From bonfires of leaves,
Conkers crack open from their protective shells,
Autumn is leaving and winter's taking over.

Lucy Dawson (10)
Mowden Junior School

Autumn!

Autumn is upon us!

Leaves somersaulting to the ground,
Sparkling through the clouds of grey.
The bare trees groan with the wind,
Endlessly howling through the sky above.

Autumn is upon us!

Conkers diving to the depths of the leaves,
That are on the floor, with another few layers.
The conkers crack like birds hatching out of their eggs.
The tears from the clouds dampen everything that gets in their way.

Autumn is upon us!

The burning and boiling planet has been taken over long ago.
Now the breath of God squirms through the treetops,
As the whining, wailing werewolf creates a gust of wind.
The leaves float silently to their new home.

Autumn is upon us!

Vermillion, russet, bronze, gold,
Copper, scarlet, brown and green.
The leaves have walked to the compost or the rake.
The first flake has fallen!

Jack Stephen Raine (10)
Mowden Junior School

Autumn

Autumn stalks through the whispering wood,
Creeping and crawling past awakening trees.
Conkers tumble swiftly to the floor,
Crashing down then cracking.

Autumn races,
Along windy paths
Dodging each tree as it rushes past
Leaping and prancing around.

Autumn lumbers along dark paths,
Leaves of all different colours,
Ruby-red, bramble-brown,
Golden, green and amber.

Stephanie Wilson (10)
Mowden Junior School

The Forest

Green giants wandering nowhere.
Bony branches clawing the air,
Winding arms reaching menacingly.

Creatures lurk secretly.
Scurrying through the heart of the forest,
Looking for food.
Guarding their homes like soldiers.

Rotting roots tripping fiendishly
Like thick ropes lying on the floor.
Russet leaves relaxing silently,
Listening to the sounds of the mighty forest.

Harry Brockbanks (10)
Mowden Junior School

Autumn!

Autumn wanders,
Listening to the trees sway in the breeze
Stepping on the golden leaves
Gazing up at the giant trees.

Autumn strolls,
Shuffling through the conkers
Wrapped up in shells,
The shell is a warm, cosy blanket.

Autumn races,
Running past the birds
Singing their song with their soft voices
They sing quietly in the trees.

Sarah Ingham (10)
Mowden Junior School

The Wind

The wind is a speedy squirrel
As it races through the trees.
Jumping from branch to branch
Leaving the trees and leaves
To whisper about him
As it moves on somewhere else.

Ben Donaldson (11)
Mowden Junior School

My Forest Poem

The trees are giants towering high,
You feel them looking, staring down,
The sun sparkling through the trees,
The russet leaves crackle noisily on the forest floor,
The wind rustles through the leaves pushing them round,
The golden branches crunch and snap as you tread on them,
Animals rustle through piles of leaves,
Spider webs glisten like diamonds with silver,
Birds chirp and chatter, singing their song,
Rivers trickle through the peaceful forests.
It smells of fresh dew and flowers,
Fungi surrounds you in their beautiful colours,
Lush green grass, cold and damp with rain
Feet sink into thick brown mud,
Then as night draws on the forest slowly dies.

Ellie May (10)
Mowden Junior School

Deep In The Forest

In the forest you can hear the rustling of the trees
                                        and the birds singing
And the smell of the damp moss.
You can see the different ranges of fungi, across the forest floor.
Lying peacefully, not making a sound.
Look at the lake, like a mirror's reflection flowing across the land.
As still as a log.
See the trees as straight as a sentry on his way.
Hear the squelch of mud underfoot.
The gills of fungi sunbathe under a glimmering sunset.
Now is the time of day when the sun starts to set.
Fungi and moss go to sleep under the tall and dying trees.
The moon is out and the sun is in.
The whole forest is asleep until another day.

Harriet Donald (10)
Mowden Junior School

Down In The Forest

Down in the forest there are lots of different things.
The trees waving their branches like they really know you.
The sun shining down to make the forest brighten up.
A smiling face shining over it all.
You can hear crunching leaves and breaking sticks, as people
explore the forest.
You can hear the tree groaning in the wind.
Like an angry boy groaning to his father.
The calm waters lying in its muddy bed.
The fungi everywhere and the fresh pine smell.
The forest floor lies calmly covered with sticks and stones.
Then the night arrives, everything goes to its bed and gets ready for
the next day.

Maddy Wood (10)
Mowden Junior School

Autumn Poem

The autumn crept, upon the trees
Shivering and swirling the leaves down onto the leafy bed.
Different colour crunching leaves curl up into a ball.
The plants grow fruit.
The whistling wind blows the bed of leaves on the floor.
The bonfire smells
And the beautiful colours
The conkers fall, bronze and shiny
As the sun rises every morning, autumn begins a new day.
Cracking sounds of the sleeping twigs on the muddy bed
Autumn grows colder as the days go to sleep
The smells of the bonfire,
The howling of the wind,
The dancing of the leaves
And the mist on the windows
Autumn falls asleep after all of his new work,
Ready for the next day to come.
The new day's come
With falling leaves
And new sweet smells
Flowers open up and stand talking proud.

Amy McLay (10)
Mowden Junior School

Snow

Snow is a white blanket
Covering trees and grass,
For animals to snuggle into.

Before snow goes to bed,
It gives the world an extra blanket,
To remember him by,
Until he comes again
Next year.

Jennifer English (11)
Mowden Junior School

Autumn Bird

Autumn arrives as a migrating bird,
Gliding on silky wings.
Turning to winter plumage,
Of golden and russet leaves.

Gracefully flying through the boney trees,
Carrying autumn in its pointed beak.
Sprinkling his magic over the world,
The autumn bird, so sleek.

The autumn bird is withering,
And tiring day by day.
It's time for him to nestle down,
And sleep another year away.

Isabel Walker (10)
Mowden Junior School

Autumn Poem

Autumn, very bright, golden, maroon, ruby and russet.
Autumn has conkers tumbled on a bed of leaves.
The trees are like skyscrapers scraping the sky.

Robert Lawson (10)
Mowden Junior School

Autumn Comes

Waking up at the sight of dawn,
In the bright and beautiful morn,
Crouched down behind a rock,
A little conker snuggly in its protective cocoon.

Autumn leaves dance along,
Like dancers in the moonlight,
Twirling and spinning around and around,
In the midnight breeze.

Trees catch every leaf,
That runs along in the whistling breeze,
Whispering and twittering to each other,
Wondering why everything changes.

As the time goes by,
Autumn's enemy comes along,
With its cold breeze and freezing snow,
Bringing autumn to a stop.
Creeping in comes . . . winter!

Daneille Murdock (10)
Mowden Junior School

Autumn

The leaves twirling in the wind
Dancing to the song of the birds
The russet-red cartwheeling
Gold and bronze spinning up and down
The bare tree standing like a statue
Watching the dance to the leaves
The russet-red, bronze and gold
Bow down to the audience
The leaves finish their performance
Cartwheeling off the stage of twigs
The mist rises like a curtain
The show has ended.

Sophie Gowling (10)
Mowden Junior School

Autumn And Moon

Autumn
Autumn whistles through the trees
Conkers tumbling on a cushion of leaves
While the leaves flutter on to the bed of grass.

Moon
The moon is a shiny diamond twinkling in the midnight sky.
The stars shining around their shiny moon.

Matthew West (10)
Mowden Junior School

A Forest Experience

In the middle of the forest,
Where the moss and the fungi stand and talk,
The breeze blows through bringing a sheet of leaves,
To cover the green, spongy floor.
The trees create a sanctuary,
Where they say goodbye to their ageing branches
As they gradually fall and die on the safe, damp floor.
Water trickles through the forest like a small pool of silver giving up.
The sun wakes up and breaks through the clouds,
Pushing its way through the green treetops,
As it wakes up the forest,
The forest stays, still talking, through the day.
As evening draws near,
A blanket of mist replaces the shine of the blazing sun,
The trees settle standing still as a soldier,
And the fungi stops talking,
To rest for the night.
As the forest falls asleep,
Waiting for dawn to rise again.

Erin Watson (10)
Mowden Junior School

Relationships

The stamp to the paper,
The stain to the coat,
The window to the frame,
And the sea to the boat.

Daniel Aydon (8)
Sacriston Junior School

Dog Kennings

Tail wager,
Ball burster,
Good swimmer,
Biscuit eater,
Fast runner,
Cat chaser,
Gates pusher,
Clothes sniffer.

Paige Calcutt (8)
Sacriston Junior School

Relationships

The rocket to the Earth
The pencil to the paper,
The water to the hands,
And the meteor to the crater.

Thomas West (8)
Sacriston Junior School

Autumn

Juicy blackberries growing wildly,
Yellow corn blowing gently,
Rosy apples ripening slowly,
Orange sun rising brightly,
Loud harvester digging noisily,
Cold birds flying quickly,
Golden leaves crunching loudly.

Samantha Roseberry (8)
Sacriston Junior School

Horse Kennings

Grass galloper
Hay hogger
High jumper
Hard hunter
Heavy hurdler
Cheeky biter
Fierce fighter
Apple eater
Stable stander.

Taylor-Jayne Johnson (8)
Sacriston Junior School

Relationships

The top to the bottom,
The ceiling to the floor,
The water to the cup
And the handle to the door.

The chalk to the chalkboard,
The spoon to the fork,
The chick to the chicken
And the meat to the hawk.

Matthew Buil (9)
Sacriston Junior School

Relationships

The pen to the paper,
The cheetah to the meat,
The monkey to the tree,
And the song to the beat.

The foot to the football,
The water to the cup,
The football to the goal
And the dog to the pup.

Joseph French (9)
Sacriston Junior School

Relationships

The spots to the ladybird.
The bat to the ball,
The books to the library
And the phone to the call.

The cat to the dog,
The flower to the soil,
The table to the chair
And the food to the foil.

Megan Weldon (8)
Sacriston Junior School

Relationships

The sea to the sand,
The bee to the flower,
The chairs to the table,
And the princess to the tower.

Paige Birnie (8)
Sacriston Junior School

Relationships

The cloud to the rain,
The star to the moon,
The cow to the barn,
And the bowl to the spoon.

The pen to the pencil,
The dress to the top,
The ink to the pen
And the bottle to the pop.

The flower to the petal,
The egg to the pan,
The bat to the ball
And the pop to the can.

Alexandra Campbell (9)
Sacriston Junior School

Relationships

The pool to the water,
The honey to the bees,
The sea to the sand
And the dog to the fleas.

The flower to the petal,
The sea to the sand,
The king to the queen
And the explorer to a new land.

Conor Robson (8)
Sacriston Junior School

Relationships

The chair to the floor,
The cube to the box,
The picture to the wall
And the cub to the fox.

The flower to the mud,
The person to the car,
The ladder to the floor,
And the person to the bar.

Zac Wright (8)
Sacriston Junior School

Relationships

The flowers to the field,
The clock to the wall,
The fish to the pond
And the hand to the ball.

Laura Wilkinson (8)
Sacriston Junior School

Relationships

The star to the planet,
The picture to the wall,
The pig to the cow
And the pitch to the ball.

The cub to the tiger,
The sand to the path,
The top to the bottom
And the water to the bath.

The French to the Spanish,
The juice to the cup,
The mane to the lion,
And the dog to the pup.

Joshua Beacham (8)
Sacriston Junior School

Relationships

The heart to the card,
The tower to the sky,
The breeze to the sun
And the cherry to the pie.

The horse to the grass,
The summer to the spring,
The world to the earth
And the finger to the ring.

The ear to the earring,
The trees to the air,
The wall to the ground
And the rides to the fair.

Elysia Scott (8)
Sacriston Junior School

Autumn

Rosy apples swinging slowly,
Shiny sun shimmering brightly,
Crimson leaves crunching softly,
Brown conkers dropping gently.

Sarah Lamb (8)
Sacriston Junior School

The Storm

The wild storm rages like an angry giant,
Flashing lightning bolts through the sky like fiery weapons.
As its thunderous voice booms and echoes furiously.
The wind shrieks quickly like a cheetah.
Its icy hands grip the house as tightly as a cuddle.
The rain beats furiously against the window like hailstones.
Inside the fire greets us like an oven
And we feel as warm and snug as the sun.

Tomas Bussey (11)
Sugar Hill Primary School

A School Day

At 8.55 the monster opens his jaws,
He opens and shuts like an elevator,
As I walk on the carpet it is wet,
And it unrolls like a tongue.

In the classroom the teacher,
Opens and closes her mouth like a yapping dog,
And children chat like dolphins,
While the blackboard squeaks like a mouse.

In the playground children play,
They scream and shout like baby cubs,
They have fun,
While parents escape to the pubs.

Finally the bell rings like an opera singer,
Children scutter about like little rabbits,
All happy to go home,
Where they start their dirty habits.

Aaron Hetherington (11)
Sugar Hill Primary School

The Ancient Greece Battles Of War

There's a war in Athens but who's going to win?
People are getting shot and stabbed by the king.
It looks like the Persians are good,
Because they are hitting a lot of blood.
Athens are going to have to catch up if they want to win.
They are losing a lot of blood so they are getting thin.
Athens are definitely catching up.
Whilst the Spartans have a cup.
They're having a celebration why Athens are having a war.
Why, people are dying and fainting on the floor.
Athens have won, finally they are all dead,
Well some are and some have a cracked head.

Jake Marshall (9)
Sugar Hill Primary School

Greecy Poem

Sailing ships, swords and shields,
All are waiting on battlefields.
Olympic Games with laughter and fun,
It's all happening in the sun.

Everyone wanted to
Act out plays,
But no one ever
Got their ways.

Nobody wanted
Quiet and peace,
Shouting and chattering
All in *Greece!*

Caitlin Hindle (9)
Sugar Hill Primary School

A Greek Poem

Long ago in a battle
There were horses and lots of cattle.
There was ancient money.
Don't you worry, they won't be dead
They will all fight instead.
There might have been war at your front door . . .
In Ancient Greece there was no peace.

Lois Rivers (9)
Sugar Hill Primary School

The Greek War Rhyme

In Greece there was no peace
Shouting soldiers kicking and killing.
Swords and spears were thrown
Sculptures were chipped
And whipped kids crying and dying.
Men were going mental
The country was being invaded.
The country was killing us but we won.
This is war.

Jack Smart (9)
Sugar Hill Primary School